D1311986

Slight print
Stain noted
NSN

4/24/14

Lady Gaga

ABDO
Publishing Company

Big Buddy BOOKS
Buddy Bios

by Sarah Tieck

VISIT US AT
www.abdopublishing.com

Published by ABDO Publishing Company, 8000 West 78th Street, Edina, Minnesota 55439.

Printed in the United States of America, North Mankato, Minnesota.
062011
092011

 PRINTED ON RECYCLED PAPER

Coordinating Series Editor: Rochelle Baltzer
Contributing Editors: Megan M. Gunderson, BreAnn Rumsch, Marcia Zappa
Graphic Design: Maria Hosley
Cover Photograph: *AP Photo*: Gregg DeGuire/PictureGroup via AP IMAGES.
Interior Photographs/Illustrations: *AP Photo*: Vince Bucci/PictureGroup via AP IMAGES (p. 14), Jason DeCrow
     (p. 27), Tom Donoghue/PictureGroup via AP IMAGES (p. 23), Paul Drinkwater/NBC/NBCU Photo Bank via
     AP Images (p. 25), Frank Micelotta/PictureGroup (p. 21), Leon Neal, pool (p. 19), Chris Pizzello (pp. 15, 29),
     Press Association via AP Images (p. 17), Matt Sayles (p. 29), Sipa via AP Images (p. 22); *Getty Images*: Daniel
     Boczarski/Redferns (p. 13), Larry Busacca/Getty Images for Giorgio Armani (p. 7), Fred Duval/FilmMagic
     (p. 17), Michael Loccisano/FilmMagic (p. 17), Danny Martindale/FilmMagic (p. 5); *Shutterstock*: kropic1 (p. 9),
     RonGreer.Com (p. 11).

Library of Congress Cataloging-in-Publication Data

Tieck, Sarah, 1976-
 Lady Gaga : singing sensation / Sarah Tieck.
    p. cm. -- (Big buddy biographies)
 ISBN 978-1-61783-017-4
 1. Lady Gaga--Juvenile literature. 2. Singers--United States--Biography--Juvenile literature. I. Title.
 ML3930.L13T54 2012
 782.42164092--dc23
 [B]
                                    2011018228

Lady
Gaga

Contents

Singing Star

Lady Gaga is a famous singer and songwriter. She has won awards for her hit albums and songs.

Lady Gaga is known for her creative style. She has appeared on magazine covers. And, she has been **interviewed** on popular television shows.

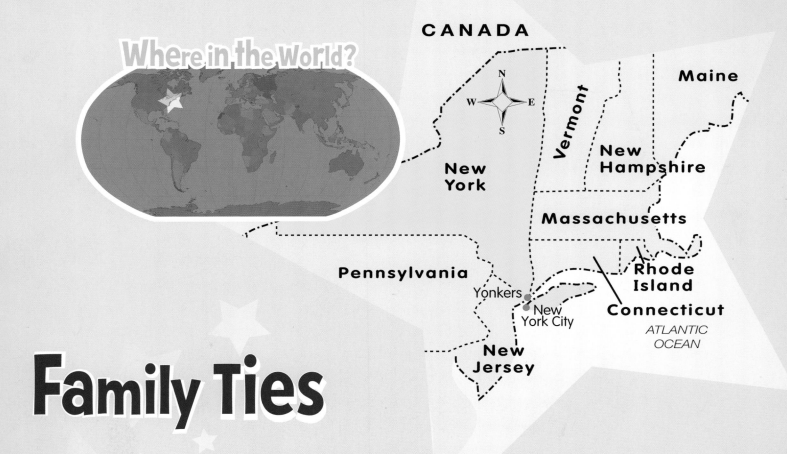

CANADA

Maine

Vermont

New York

New Hampshire

Massachusetts

Pennsylvania

Yonkers

New York City

Rhode Island

Connecticut

ATLANTIC OCEAN

New Jersey

Family Ties

Lady Gaga's real name is Stefani Joanne Angelina Germanotta. She was born in Yonkers, New York, on March 28, 1986. Her parents are Joseph and Cynthia Germanotta. Her younger sister is Natali.

When Stefani was growing up, her father had an Internet business. Her mother worked in an office.

Growing Up

Stefani grew up in New York City. As a child, she loved music. At age 4, she could play songs on the piano after simply hearing them. When she was 13, she began writing her own songs. Soon, she was performing!

At age 17, Stefani was asked to attend New York University's Tisch School of the Arts. This was a big honor.

Stefani attended high school in New York City. She studied at a private school called Convent of the Sacred Heart.

Did you know...

Stefani has always been creative. In high school, her style and clothes sometimes stood out. Stefani remembers being made fun of for this.

9

Starting Out

Stefani wanted to begin working in music. She believed that she could learn more by **performing** than by taking classes. So when she was 19, she left New York University.

Soon, Stefani was working as a singer and dancer. She even created some of her own costumes!

Did you know...

Stefani's dad made her promise to return to school if she hadn't found success in music by age 20.

Lady Gaga performed as often as she could. She liked wearing flashy clothes!

Big Break

Around 2006, Stefani got a job writing songs for other singers. Still, she wanted to be a singer herself. So, she kept writing and **performing** her own music.

People soon noticed Stefani's talent. She took the name Lady Gaga. And, she changed her look.

In 2008, Lady Gaga **released** her first album. It is called *The Fame*. Songs on *The Fame* have a strong dance beat. "Just Dance" and "Poker Face" became hits around the world!

Lady Gaga worked on many parts of *The Fame*. She wrote the songs and music. And, she played instruments and sang.

In 2010, Lady Gaga won two Grammy Awards for her work on *The Fame*.

Lady Gaga often has many costume changes at events.

Fashion Plate

Lady Gaga is known for her unusual clothes. Some looks are **inspired** by news events, holidays, or her songs. Others come from Lady Gaga's beliefs and ideas. Sometimes she just wears things she finds interesting.

Many of Lady Gaga's outfits are fancy leotards. She often pairs them with belts, high heels, and sunglasses.

Lady Gaga wears different wigs and dyes her hair to give herself new looks.

In 2010, Lady Gaga wore a dress made of raw meat. She even had a matching purse and shoes!

Lady Gaga's music has made her famous. She has met many famous people. In 2009, she met Queen Elizabeth II of England!

New Opportunities

Lady Gaga gained many fans. In 2009, she **released** her second major album. It is called *The Fame Monster*. Lady Gaga wrote many of this album's songs about her life and ideas.

Fans loved *The Fame Monster*. It had several hit songs including "Telephone" and "Bad Romance." The album and its songs won several awards. Three were **Grammy Awards**!

Lady Gaga recorded "Telephone" with famous singer Beyoncé (*right*).

A Singer's Life

Lady Gaga works hard on her music. She writes songs for her albums. Then, she spends many hours recording her music.

Lady Gaga also goes on concert tours. Her shows include **dramatic** and colorful costumes. There is dancing, too. So, Lady Gaga must plan and practice before **performing**.

Lady Gaga likes over-the-top shows. She says she spends the money she earns to improve them.

23

When she is on tour, Lady Gaga may spend months away from home. She travels to cities around the world and **performs** live concerts. She also attends events and meets fans. Her fans are often excited to see her!

In 2011, Lady Gaga appeared on
The Tonight Show with Jay Leno.

25

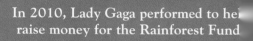

In 2010, Lady Gaga performed to he[lp] raise money for the Rainforest Fund.

Off the Stage

When Lady Gaga has free time, she visits her friends and family. She also likes to help people and **charities**. She is interested in making sure all people have the same rights.

Buzz

Lady Gaga's fame continues to grow. In 2011, she **released** her third major album. It is called *Born This Way*.

People are often surprised by Lady Gaga's changing style. Fans are excited to see what's next for her. Many believe Lady Gaga has a bright **future**!

In 2011, Lady Gaga sang at the Grammy Awards (*above*). Earlier, she had surprised people by arriving in an egg-like pod (*right*)!

29

Web sites
links page. These links are routinely
updated to provide the most current information available.

www.abdopublishing.com

A CHILDREN'S CHRISTMAS CAROL
"O COME, LITTLE CHILDREN"

1st E♭ Alto Saxophone

J.A.P. Schulz/Magill

A Children's Christmas Carol
"O Come, Little Children"

2nd E♭ Alto Saxophone

J.A.P. Schulz/Magill

O Come, Little Children was composed by Johann Abraham Peter Schulz (b.1747 - d.1800). Schulz was the court composer at Rheinsberg, Germany and a choir director for the Royal Court Theater in Copenhagen, Denmark. He was best known for setting poems to simple, folk-like music. The German poet, Christoph von Schmid, wrote the words to this song.

THE FRIENDLY BEASTS

1st E♭ Alto Saxophone

Medieval French Melody

THE FRIENDLY BEASTS

2nd E♭ Alto Saxophone

Medieval French Melody

The melody for **The Friendly Beasts** dates back to 12th century medieval France while the words were written at a later date. **The Friendly Beasts** is usually thought of as an old English carol.

RIO BRAVO

1st E♭ Alto Saxophone

RIO BRAVO

2nd E♭ Alto Saxophone

Latin America is made up of South America, Central America, Mexico, and the West Indies. The music of this region is a combination of Spanish, Portuguese, and Italian traditions and has been influenced by the cultures of the native Indians like the Aztec, Incan, and Mayan. It features catchy melodies, infectious rhythms, and a wide use of percussion instruments.

W26XE

BIG ROCK CANDY MOUNTAIN

1st E♭ Alto Saxophone

Traditional American Folk

BIG ROCK CANDY MOUNTAIN

2nd E♭ Alto Saxophone

Traditional American Folk

Folk songs are passed down from generation to generation through singing and listening. The common folk sing the songs to their children instead of writing them down. The original composers were forgotten as time passed and the words and places changed. These changes left many versions of the same song. **Big Rock Candy Mountain** originated in the late 1800's and was attributed to Harry "Haywire Mac" McClintock. The ballad tells of a hobo's life, riding the trains and traveling the country, in search of the perfect place for a "burly bum" to live.

ROYAL CROWN MARCH

1st E♭ Alto Saxophone

ROYAL CROWN MARCH

2nd Eb Alto Saxophone

The history of the march has its beginnings in the military. Marches have a steady beat that is strongly accented. This beat was helpful for soldiers to stay in step. Many marches were written to commemorate a regal occasion such as the crowning of a king. It was with this in mind that **Royal Crown March** was composed.

W26XE

7

BOOT SCOOTIN' BARN DANCE

Ron Cowherd
Traditional American Folk

1st E♭ Alto Saxophone

W26XE

©1985 Kjos West. Used with permission.

BOOT SCOOTIN' BARN DANCE

Ron Cowherd
Traditional American Folk

2nd Eb Alto Saxophone

A significant part of a country's heritage and culture is found in its folk music. Using the language of the common folk, folk songs describe the lives and times of its people. This piece uses the folk song, **Ol' Joe Clark.** Joe Clark was a veteran from the war of 1812 who lived in the Appalachian Mountains. The numerous verses were made up from incidents in his life and expanded as time passed to include over 90 different verses.

W26XE

8

BAG O' BLUES

1st E♭ Alto Saxophone

BAG O' BLUES

2nd E♭ Alto Saxophone

The blues is a style of music developed from the African-American field hollers, work songs, and spirituals of the late 1800's to early 1900's. It is played at a slow to moderate tempo and usually written in 4/4 time. The third, fifth, and seventh notes of the scale in which the piece is written are lowered one half-step.

W26XE

9

A LITTLE BIT OF LATIN

1st E♭ Alto Saxophone

A Little Bit of Latin

2nd E♭ Alto Saxophone

The music of Latin America, influenced by the many cultures and traditions of its people, uses lively rhythms for dances like the habanera, rumba, cha-cha, and tango. The music uses many percussion instruments such as the claves, maracas, and cowbell to keep the rhythm.

W26XE

A Classical Canon

1st E♭ Alto Saxophone

Franz Joseph Haydn/Magill

A Classical Canon

2nd E♭ Alto Saxophone

Franz Joseph Haydn/Magill

Franz Joseph Haydn (b.1732 - d.1809) was an Austrian composer who worked as the court composer for the royal Esterhazy family for over thirty years. "Papa Haydn," best known for his numerous symphonies and string quartets, also trained and conducted the other court musicians. **A Classical Canon** was originally called the *Nightingale Canon*. Words were added later describing children's anticipation to stay up on Christmas Eve while the parent sang for the children to go to bed. The title then became commonly known as the *Christmas Eve Canon*.

DR. ROCK

1st E♭ Alto Saxophone

Chuck Elledge

DR. ROCK

2nd Eb Alto Saxophone

Chuck Elledge

Rock music evolved into a distinctive style of music with songs like *Rock Around the Clock* and *You Ain't Nothin' But a Hound Dog*. During the 1960's, a British band called the Beatles became very popular. In the 1970's and 1980's, electronic instruments and advanced recording techniques were developed to enhance the music.

12

FANFARE AND MINUET FROM
"THE ROYAL FIREWORKS"

1st E♭ Alto Saxophone

George Frideric Handel

FANFARE AND MINUET FROM
"THE ROYAL FIREWORKS"

2nd E♭ Alto Saxophone

George Frideric Handel

George Frideric Handel (b.1685 - d.1759) was a popular German composer who traveled widely throughout his life and settled in England. The English royalty paid him well for his many compositions. The **Music for the Royal Fireworks**, written in 1749, originally called for a huge ensemble of brass, woodwinds, timpani, and a cannon. Handel wrote the piece to accompany a fireworks celebration for the King of England. Just as the music began, the fireworks exploded accidentally. In spite of the accident, Handel's piece was a great success.

BOOGIE BLUES

13

1st E♭ Alto Saxophone

BOOGIE BLUES

2nd E♭ Alto Saxophone

Blues music evolved throughout the early 20th century. "Boogie-woogie," a popular style developed during this time, was normally played at a fast tempo, had a repeated melodic pattern in the bass (called a "walking bass"), swinging eighth notes, and a series of improvised variations in the upper melody.

W26XE

MINOR ROCK

1st E♭ Alto Saxophone

MINOR ROCK

2nd E♭ Alto Saxophone

"Rock and Roll" was a phrase used by disk jockey, Allan Freed, in the early 1950's. He wanted to attract teenagers to his Rhythm and Blues concerts. The name caught on and rock and roll replaced American "pop" music. Rock music has a heavy dance beat with strong accents on beats 2 and 4 and lyrics that relate well to young people.

W26XE

GLOSSARY

Accent > . . . . play the beginning of the note louder

Accidentals ♯, ♭, ♮ . . . . sharp, flat, or natural

Allegro . . . . quick and lively

Andante . . . . moderately slow

Articulation . . . . type of attack used to play a note or group of notes

Bar Line ≣ . . . . divides the music staff into measures

Bass Clef 𝄢 . . . . F Clef, read by bassoon, trombone, baritone, tuba, timpani, and electric bass

Blues . . . . American genre of popular vocal music, developed from African-American field hollers, work songs, and spirituals; characterized by a harmonic structure that is made up of a 12-measure phrase

Breath Mark ' . . . . take a breath

Canon . . . . a style of contrapuntal music, similar to a round

Carol . . . . song usually associated with Christmas

Common Time 𝄴 . . . . same as 4/4

Crescendo ⟨ . . . . gradually play louder

Decrescendo ⟩ . . . . gradually play softer

Double Bar ≣▌ . . . . marks the end of the music

Dynamics . . . . loudness or softness of music

Fermata ⌒ . . . . hold note or rest longer than its usual value

Flat ♭ . . . . lowers the pitch of a note by a half step

Forte *f* . . . . loud

Fortissimo *ff* . . . . very loud

Harmony . . . . result of two or more different notes played or sung at the same time

Improvise . . . . to create music as it is being performed

Jazz . . . . style of American popular music that emerged at the turn of the 20th century and continued to evolve throughout the 20th century

Key Signature . . . . sharps or flats stated right after the clef; key signatures change certain notes throughout a piece of music

Ledger Lines ≣ . . . . short lines added above or below the staff used to extend the staff to notate pitches that are beyond the range of the staff

Long Rest ⊢4⊣ . . . . rest the number of measures indicated

Maestoso . . . . majestically

Measure ≣ . . . . space between two bar lines; also known as a "bar"

Medieval . . . . (also known as Middle Ages, 400-1400AD) a time in European history of warfare, religious devotion, and royal pageantry

Melody . . . . organized succession of tones

Mezzo Forte *mf* . . . . medium loud

Mezzo Piano *mp* . . . . medium soft

Moderato . . . . moderate speed

Natural ♮ . . . . cancels a flat or sharp

One-Measure Repeat ⁄ . . . . . . repeat the previous measure

Percussion Clef ≣ . . . . indicates that the lines and spaces on the staff do not designate specific pitches; also called neutral clef or no-pitch clef; read by snare drum, bass drum, cymbals, and most other auxiliary percussion instruments

Phrase . . . . musical thought or sentence

Piano *p* . . . . soft

Pick-Up Note(s) ≣ . . . . note or notes that come before the first full measure of a piece

Popular Music . . . . music of everyday life, it has played a role in each historical period

Repeat Sign ≣ . . . . repeat from beginning or repeat the section of music between repeat signs

Rhythm and Blues . . . . American style of popular music often described as an urban style of blues; instrumentation included drums, piano, electric guitar and bass, saxophone, brass, and vocalists

Rock . . . . style of American popular music that developed in the 1960's from rock and roll, with more amplification and distortion of sound and more room for improvisation

Rock and Roll . . . . style of American popular music that developed from rhythm and blues in the 1950's and was especially popular among young people

Sharp ♯ . . . . raises the pitch of a note 1/2 step

Slur ♩♩ . . . . curved line connecting two or more notes of different pitches

Solo/Soli . . . . one person plays/whole section plays

Staccato ♩ . . . . dot placed above or below a note meaning to play short and detached

Staff ≣ . . . . lines and spaces on which music is written

Swing . . . . style of American popular music that was played by the "big bands" of the 1930's and 1940's

Tempo . . . . speed of music

Tenuto ♩ . . . . line placed above or below a note meaning to sustain for full value

Tie ♩♩ . . . . curved line that connects two notes on the same line or space

Time Signature 4/4 3/4 2/4 . . . . . . top number tells the number of counts in each measure; bottom number tells the type of note that receives one count

Treble Clef 𝄞 . . . . G Clef; read by flute, oboe, clarinets, saxophones, trumpet, French horn, and mallet percussion

Two-Measure Repeat ≣ . . repeat the two previous measures